THIS JOURNAL BELONGS TO:

Created by Dawn Harris
Founder of Budget Me Crazy

MONTHLY CALENDAR

SUN	MON	TUE	WED

THUR	FRI	SAT	$
			_____
			_____
			_____
			_____
			_____
			_____
			_____
			_____
			_____
			_____
			_____
			_____
			_____

$

Month Of:

Pay Date(s):	Amount:

Totals:

Type:	Amount:
Income:	
Expenses:	
Remaining:	

Date	Bill Description	Category	Amount	Paid

Savings Tracker

Date	Account	Activity	Balance

$

No Spend Challenge:

Try to only spend on necessities for at least one week during this month.

Debt Tracker

Date	Account	Category	Amount

MONTHLY CALENDAR

SUN	MON	TUE	WED

THUR	FRI	SAT	$

$

Month Of:

Pay Date(s):	Amount:

Totals:

Type:	Amount:
Income:	
Expenses:	
Remaining:	

Date	Bill Description	Category	Amount	Paid

Savings Tracker

Date	Account	Activity	Balance

$

Eat at Home Challenge:

Try to only make meals at home during this month.

Debt Tracker

Date	Account	Category	Amount

MONTHLY CALENDAR

SUN	MON	TUE	WED

THUR	FRI	SAT	
			$
			_____
			_____
			_____
			_____
			_____
			_____
			_____
			_____
			_____
			_____
			_____
			_____

$

Month Of:

Income:

Pay Date(s):	Amount:

Totals:

Type:	Amount:
Income:	
Expenses:	
Remaining:	

Date	Bill Description	Category	Amount	Paid

Savings Tracker

Date	Account	Activity	Balance

$

Credit Card Challenge:

For 30 days, don't use a credit card for any purchases.

Debt Tracker

Date	Account	Category	Amount

MONTHLY CALENDAR

SUN	MON	TUE	WED

THUR	FRI	SAT	$

$

Month Of:

Income:

Pay Date(s):	Amount:

Totals:

Type:	Amount:
Income:	
Expenses:	
Remaining:	

Date	Bill Description	Category	Amount	Paid

Savings Tracker

Date	Account	Activity	Balance

$

Spending Challenge:

For 30 days, track every single dime you spend.

Debt Tracker

Date	Account	Category	Amount

MONTHLY CALENDAR

SUN	MON	TUE	WED

THUR	FRI	SAT	$
			_____
			_____
			_____
			_____
			_____
			_____
			_____
			_____
			_____
			_____
			_____
			_____
			_____
			_____

$

Month Of:

Income:

Pay Date(s):	Amount:

Totals:

Type:	Amount:
Income:	
Expenses:	
Remaining:	

Date	Bill Description	Category	Amount	Paid

Savings Tracker

Date	Account	Activity	Balance

$

No Spend Challenge:

Try only to spend on necessities for at least two weeks during this month.

Debt Tracker

Date	Account	Category	Amount

MONTHLY CALENDAR

SUN	MON	TUE	WED

THUR	FRI	SAT	
			$
			_____
			_____
			_____
			_____
			_____
			_____
			_____
			_____
			_____
			_____
			_____
			_____
			_____
			_____

Income: ——————— **Totals:** ———————

$

Month Of:

Pay Date(s):	Amount:		Type:	Amount:
			Income:	
			Expenses:	
			Remaining:	

Date	Bill Description	Category	Amount	Paid

Savings Tracker

Date	Account	Activity	Balance
_____	_____	_____	_____
_____	_____	_____	_____
_____	_____	_____	_____
_____	_____	_____	_____
_____	_____	_____	_____
_____	_____	_____	_____
_____	_____	_____	_____

$

Cash Only Challenge:

Continue to pay your fixed bills by debit or auto-withdrawal, but try to use cash for regular daily purchases.

Debt Tracker

Date	Account	Category	Amount
_____	_____	_____	_____
_____	_____	_____	_____
_____	_____	_____	_____
_____	_____	_____	_____
_____	_____	_____	_____
_____	_____	_____	_____

MONTHLY CALENDAR

SUN	MON	TUE	WED

THUR	FRI	SAT	
			$

$

Month Of:

Income:

Pay Date(s):	Amount:

Totals:

Type:	Amount:
Income:	
Expenses:	
Remaining:	

Date	Bill Description	Category	Amount	Paid

Savings Tracker

Date	Account	Activity	Balance

$

Spare Change Challenge:

Set aside the change from each purchase, putting it into a jar or savings account.

Debt Tracker

Date	Account	Category	Amount

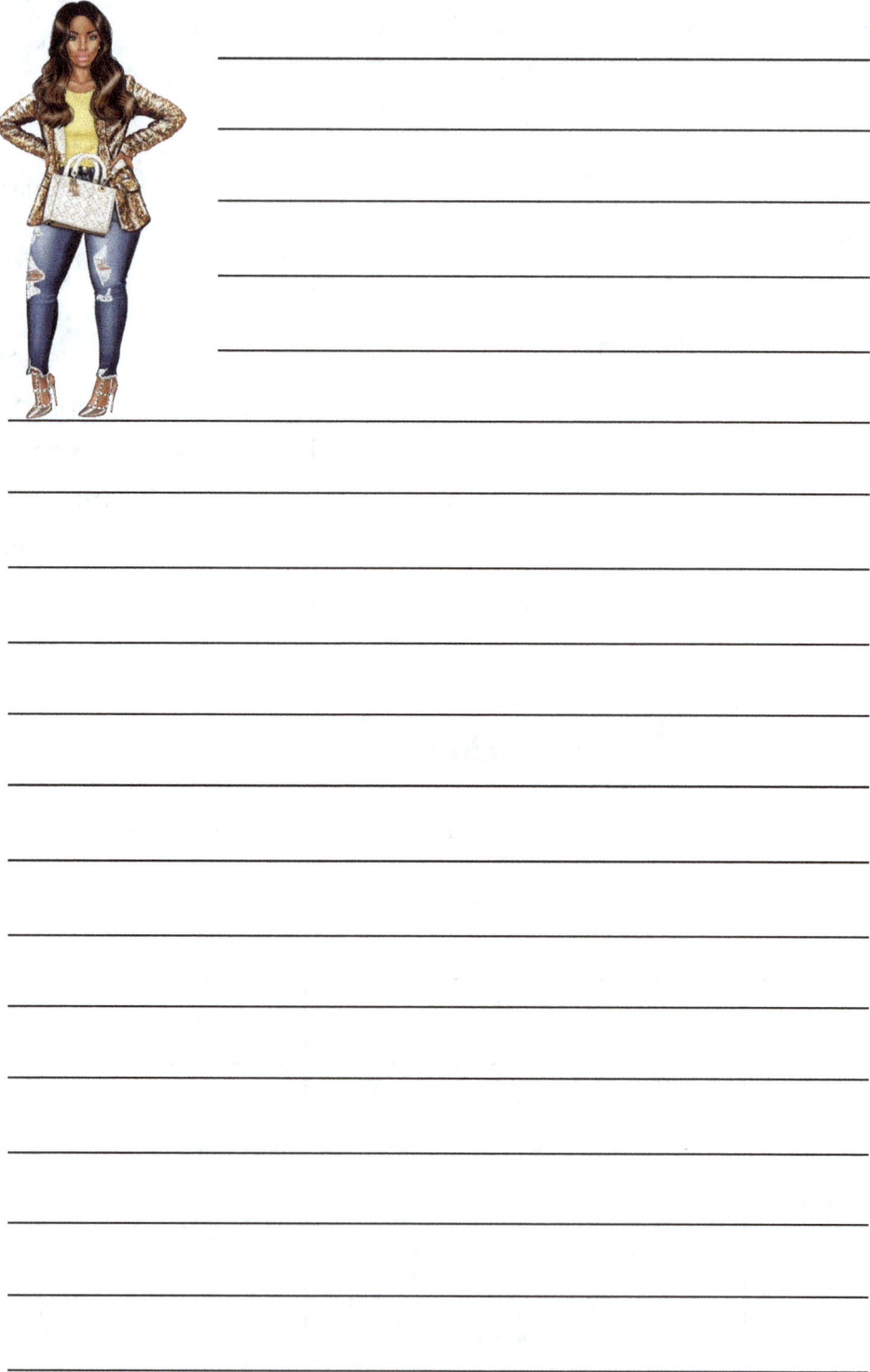

MONTHLY CALENDAR

SUN	MON	TUE	WED

THUR	FRI	SAT	
			$
			_____
			_____
			_____
			_____
			_____
			_____
			_____
			_____
			_____
			_____
			_____
			_____
			_____

$

Month Of:

Income:

Pay Date(s):	Amount:

Totals:

Type:	Amount:
Income:	
Expenses:	
Remaining:	

Date	Bill Description	Category	Amount	Paid

Savings Tracker

Date	Account	Activity	Balance

$

No Spend Challenge

Try only to spend on necessities for at least one week during this month.

Debt Tracker

Date	Account	Category	Amount

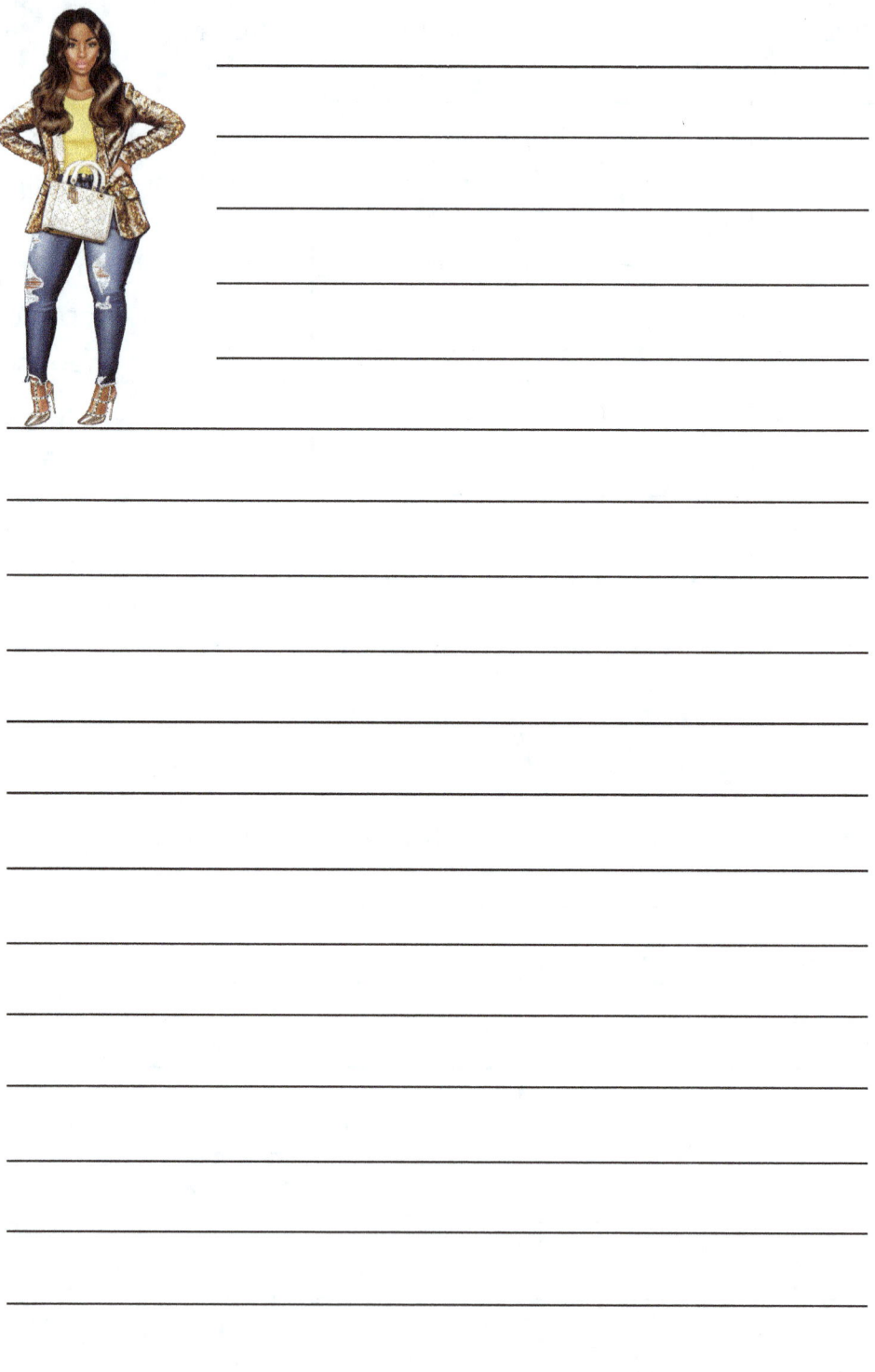

MONTHLY CALENDAR

SUN	MON	TUE	WED

THUR	FRI	SAT	
			$
			____
			____
			____
			____
			____
			____
			____
			____
			____
			____
			____
			____
			____

$

Month Of:

Pay Date(s):	Amount:

Totals:

Type:	Amount:
Income:	
Expenses:	
Remaining:	

Date	Bill Description	Category	Amount	Paid

Savings Tracker

Date	Account	Activity	Balance

$

Eat at Home Challenge

Try to only make meals at home during this month.

Debt Tracker

Date	Account	Category	Amount

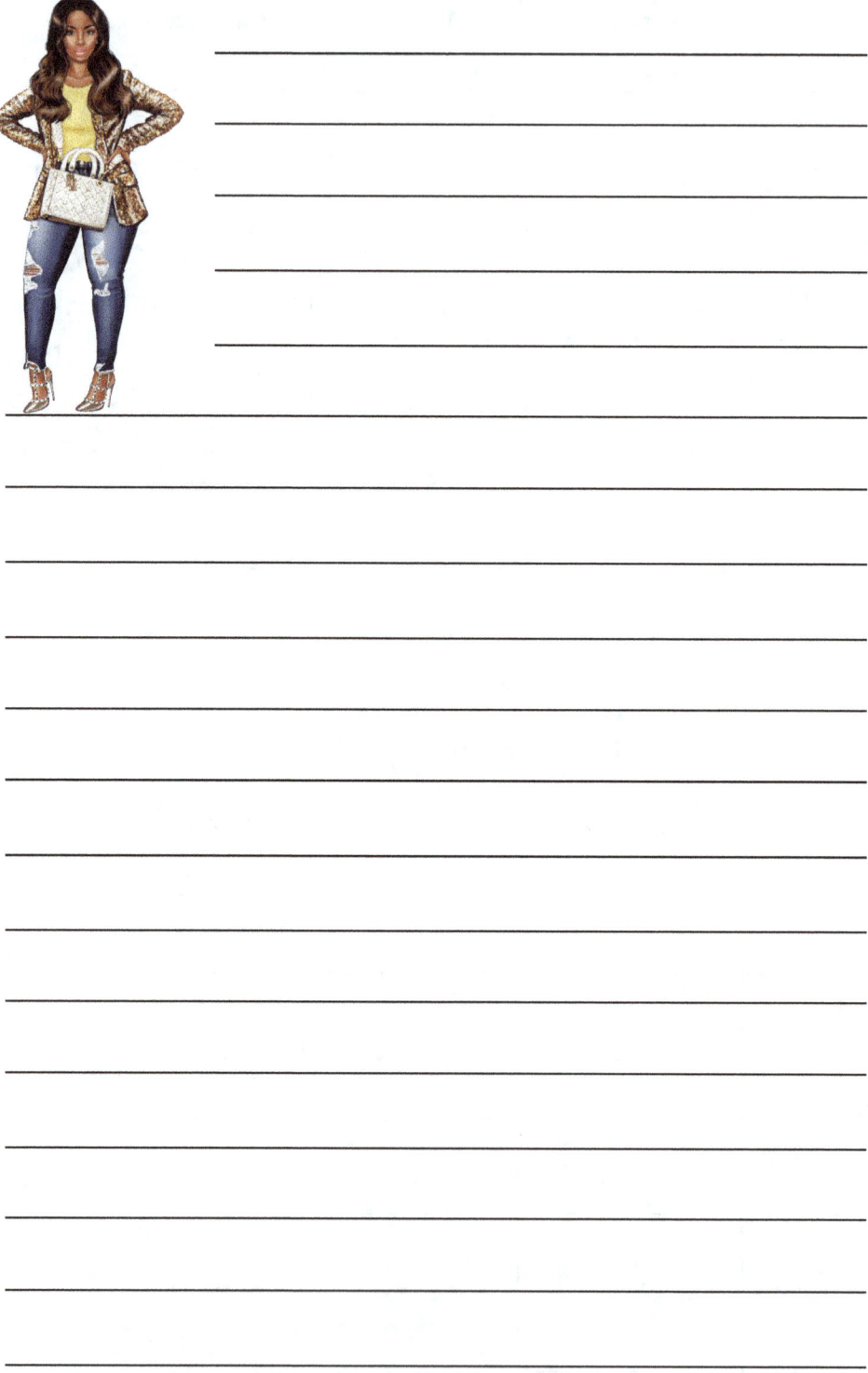

MONTHLY CALENDAR

SUN	MON	TUE	WED

THUR	FRI	SAT	
			$
			_____
			_____
			_____
			_____
			_____
			_____
			_____
			_____
			_____
			_____
			_____
			_____

$

Month Of:

Income:

Pay Date(s):	Amount:

Totals:

Type:	Amount:
Income:	
Expenses:	
Remaining:	

Date	Bill Description	Category	Amount	Paid

Savings Tracker

Date	Account	Activity	Balance

$

Credit Card Challenge

For 30 days, don't use a credit card for any purchases.

Debt Tracker

Date	Account	Category	Amount

MONTHLY CALENDAR

SUN	MON	TUE	WED

THUR	FRI	SAT	
			$

$

Month Of:

Income:

Pay Date(s):	Amount:

Totals:

Type:	Amount:
Income:	
Expenses:	
Remaining:	

Date	Bill Description	Category	Amount	Paid

Savings Tracker

Date	Account	Activity	Balance

$

Spending Challenge

For 30 days, track every single dime you spend.

Debt Tracker

Date	Account	Category	Amount

MONTHLY CALENDAR

SUN	MON	TUE	WED

THUR	FRI	SAT	
			$
			_____
			_____
			_____
			_____
			_____
			_____
			_____
			_____
			_____
			_____
			_____
			_____
			_____

$

Month Of:

Income:

Pay Date(s):	Amount:

Totals:

Type:	Amount:
Income:	
Expenses:	
Remaining:	

Date	Bill Description	Category	Amount	Paid

Savings Tracker

Date	Account	Activity	Balance

$

No Spend Challenge

Try only to spend on necessities for at least two weeks during this month.

Debt Tracker

Date	Account	Category	Amount

Helpful Money Calcuations

20-30-50 – Budgeting Ratio

- 20% should be immediately saved (goals or retirement) or put towards paying down debt
- 30% should be the maximum you spend on housing.
- 50% should be spent on everything else.

Personal Net Worth

- Personal net worth is a measurement of an individuals' total wealth. It is calculated as the tot value of all your assets minus the total value of all your liabilities.

Net Worth = Total Assets – Total Liabilities

Credit Utilization Ratio

- Measures how much credit you're using compared to how much you have available.

$$\frac{\text{Credit Balance}}{\text{Credit Limit}} \text{ (x) } 100 = \text{Credit Utilization Ratio}$$

Debt to Income Ratio (DTI)

- Calculates how much of your monthly income is devoted to debt payments.

$$\text{Debt to Income Ratio} = \frac{\text{Total Recurring Debt}}{\text{Gross Monthly Income}}$$

The Rule of 72

- A simple formula that tells you how long it will take for your money or investments to double in value

$$\frac{72}{\text{Interest Rate}} = \text{Time to double your investment}$$

Check out www.Budgetmecrazy.com for more financial tips.